That Day

My Story of September 11th

JEAN COLAIO

ISBN: 1499182112
ISBN 13: 9781499182118
Library of Congress Control Number: 2014907361
CreateSpace Independent Publishing Platform
North Charleston, South Carolina

This book is dedicated to the memory of my late brothers,
Mark Joseph Colaio and Stephen John Colaio.

Contents

Introduction vii

PART ONE: MY STORY OF THAT DAY

Chapter 1   The Beginning: Colaio History 1

Chapter 2   That Day: September 11th—A Morning of Confusion and Terror...9

Chapter 3   That Afternoon: The Towers Are Down; Where Do We Go Now? 17

Chapter 4   That Evening: It Was an Act of Terrorism...........21

Chapter 5   The Next Morning: Our Temporary Residence....23

Chapter 6   The Next Afternoon: The Search Begins 25

Chapter 7   The Next Evening: The Gathering of DNA 27

Chapter 8   Two Days After: Morning—The Most Supportive Friends Surround Us 31

Chapter 9   Two Days After: Afternoon—The Cantor Relief Center 33

Chapter 10   Three Days After: Horrible Discovery 37

Chapter 11   Four Days After: Funeral Arrangements.............41

Chapter 12   Nine Days After: Final Good-byes.......................43

Chapter 13   Four Months Later: The Holidays........................ 45

Chapter 14   One Year Later: Anniversary Day 47

PART TWO: REFLECTIONS

Reflections 59

There Are Good People in the World 60

There Are Evil People in the World 62

People Grieve Differently 63

Different Groups Form during Grieving................................ 65

Many People Have Been Struck by
Tragedy in Some Way 67

Faith Ultimately Can Get You Through 68

Good Can Come from Tragedy 70

PART THREE MARK AND STEPHEN COLAIO
MEMORIALIZED

Legacy.com Guest Book 79

Acknowledgments... 89

Introduction

I really don't want to remember any of it, but it's become a part of me. Thirteen years have passed, and I'm just now, finally, taking a deeper look at what happened. It comes to me so vividly at times, even though I've tried to discard that day from my memory. They say flashbacks are what soldiers experience when they come home from war. Well, I declare September 11th to be a day of war—a war on innocents who had been conducting their daily lives in the financial hub of the world. On that day, who would have thought it would be their last? How could it have happened, really? Men, women, mothers, fathers, sons, sisters—and in my case, two brothers—perished that day. This is hard to imagine; all these victims had been so unaware. Pick up a bagel, a cup of coffee, and take your last elevator trip up to the 104th floor of the World Trade Center's North Tower.

I try not to think of my brothers in the office on that day. That's a very dark place for me. There's footage of people gasping for air, or jumping. Every picture looks as if it could be of my brothers...dying. Imagine, there are pictures of people taking their last breaths—for the world to see. How can this even be? There are so many stories from that day, but I need to put mine into words. This event was so public; everyone shared this tragedy with my family and me that day. That day...the worst of my life.

PART ONE

My Story of That Day

CHAPTER 1

The Beginning: Colaio History

Our family grew up in a middle-class New York City suburb on Long Island. Hicksville treated us well; it was made up of good, honest, hardworking people, and many families shared the same values we did. My father is of Italian descent, and my mother came off the boat from Ireland. We were raised Catholic and never missed a week of church in Hicksville at St. Ignatius Loyola Church; my parents instilled our Catholic beliefs by word and role modeling. They're two of the most decent, honest, genuine people I've ever known.

My brothers and I remained close throughout our lives; we were one another's confidants and had very fun, fulfilling lives together. We shared many experiences growing up and were involved in one another's lives. We listened to Billy Joel and frequented the Mid-Island Shopping Plaza and Cantiague Park. My father was my brothers' little league coach, and I sat on the sidelines to take statistics. On Saturdays my father took us into the city to the Downtown Athletic Club for the Sons and Daughters of Members sports program. Sports became very important to my brothers and me, especially because it was something we could share. It was this activity, being a part of the program, that made us appreciate athletics and New York City all in one fell swoop. The three of us looked forward to the calisthenics as well as the swim meets at the DAC pool. The best part was the lunches afterward; we always ate the greatest hamburgers and fries in the city, although after a morning of rigorous athletics, any meal would be the best in the world.

At home we led very stable, normal existences. My mother, Mary Christina, was a traditional mom in every sense. She stayed home and cared for her children, and she encouraged us to put our all into any endeavor, especially academics. She pushed us to complete our homework and to get good grades and to do well in everything we tried, while she cooked wonderful traditional Irish meals and maintained the household.

My mother left Tralee, Ireland, when she was sixteen in 1954. She had thirteen brothers and sisters to contend with, so as soon as she had the chance, she was off to London. There she worked for several years before arriving on the *Queen Mary* in New York, where she found a job caring for the children of a wealthy family in Brooklyn. A few years later, she and my father met at an Irish dance on Eighty-Sixth Street and two years later were married. They celebrated at Hotel St. George in Brooklyn, which overlooks downtown NYC. They moved to Long Island and had the three of us. My mother always wanted better for her children; therefore she stressed the importance of education for us. If we did well, followed rules, and received a good education, she considered that a true accomplishment.

My father, Victor, provided us with tremendous guidance and a decent, honest moral system that served my brothers and me well in life. He was the "softie" when it came to disciplining, but I never knew a man who was so "even Steven," "steady Eddie" in all areas. He grew up in Little Italy in New York City and had seen it all. He even wrote a book about his experiences there, *Between Two Bridges*. I always remember him working hard. The long hours he put in at his job as an NYC fireman weren't uncommon when we were young. My brothers and I anxiously waited for his return home so we could put on his fire-fighter boots. We'd try on his gear and play "rescue" whenever we could.

My father was an accountant as well. When I was older, I used to tell him he had a blue collar/white collar identity struggle. He explained that his father, who was a hero to him, had been a NYC police officer. He wanted to identify with his father, thus working as a fireman, but also needed another interesting job, that of an accountant. Really, he represented the best of both worlds. My father worked hard and landed a job on Wall Street in a securities firm. Our suburban bubble burst; we were now exposed to an entirely different world. Perks we'd never seen before became common—bonuses, car service, meals at the nicest restaurants in the city, great seats at top concerts, lavish parties, and much more. We came from a humble background, and once my father started on Wall Street in 1983, we saw a new world, although we always maintained our Hicksville roots.

In college I worked on Fulton Street with my father at RMJ Securities during every break from school. I worked in the early 1980's which was an exciting time on Wall Street. People worked hard in the day and played hard at night. The owners were exceptional men who had been in the business for some years, and they treated my father and me as they did their other employees—with respect. My father went on to run the firm's London and Tokyo offices, which broadened our family's horizons even further.

My brothers also were mixed into the fold; nepotism ruled in this business. Mark, who was witty and intelligent, had graduated from high school, tried out the firm for a summer, with the plan to eventually go to college. He happened to find his niche immediately. He had the job of inputting the hundreds of different trades that the brokers provided as they yelled across the trading floor. He was a natural, able to handle different stimuli all at once (which was reminiscent of our old game-room days at the Mid-Island Plaza). For some reason he was able to focus more than others, and by age twenty-two, he was the head of the agency desk. He also really cared about the people he worked with. Mark always described work as being a "big game," and his team players had to work together. He was able to carry over his athletic-leadership abilities and core values to Wall Street, which was one of the reasons he was so successful.

Stephen, who was gregarious and amusing, was the youngest of us three Colaio siblings, also worked at the firm during his college breaks. He started in the coffee room, collecting fifty cents per cup from his coworkers. He sold a heck of a lot of coffee. Stephen loved it, since he genuinely enjoyed talking to and learning about people. He had a very special quality of making people feel good about themselves, through giving them compliments or making them laugh with a ridiculously funny story. He had been voted most popular, class clown, class flirt and Prom King of his high school. Stephen definitely lit up the room with his charm. Stephen eventually moved to a desk job there and then, after graduating from college, landed a job with another financial company.

After college, I worked for three years on the short-bond desk. I was taught by the best in the business, Mark. The job was OK while it lasted, but then I realized the financial industry wasn't for me. In the end I returned to New York University to earn a master's degree in counseling psychology. It was the best thing for me, as I'd always wanted to work in an educational setting. Wall Street had its allure, but I felt it was time for a change.

Over the next few years, I worked at NYU then at a wonderful New York City private school. Stephen was doing well at Paine Webber for a time, and after a few years, Mark was lured away to a competitor, Cantor Fitzgerald, where he ran the agency desk and had more responsibility. He hired people he had known; they were terrific employees and friends. It usually went like this:

"Do you know anyone who could fit in here who has business experience?" "Sure, Mark. I have a brother [or brother-in-law or sister or friend or roommate]."

"Bring them in."

Or:

"Hey, Mark. I have a nephew who's looking for summer work."

"Sure, we'll find something for him. Bring him on down."

In 1998 Mark asked Stephen to come work with him. Stephen did and was very successful in the position of an agency broker. Mark asked me to work with him in the fall of 2000. I turned him down, though, telling him I loved working at my school and couldn't leave the position.

"Jean, come work with me for five years," he said. "You'll be able to pay for your son's college. You live down the block—you can leave at five every day. Be with us."

I considered his offer, but I believed in what I did and loved the families of the students I worked with as well as the school.

"I can't. I have students I'd disappoint. I'm working at a great place," I told him. Mark was disappointed but understood.

One of the last great gatherings of friends and family before that fateful day was Stephen's thirty-first surprise birthday party in SoHo. He couldn't get over the fact that Mark and I hadn't done anything special for his thirtieth birthday. We had to make up for the year of jabs and managed to completely surprise our younger brother. Everyone wore a throwback picture of Stephen on his or her lapel to properly embarrass him. Speeches and memories were made. It would be his last birthday party.

Fast-forward to 2001. Mark was married to his lovely wife, June, and had a beautiful daughter, Delaney (almost three) and a son, Joseph (nineteen months old). I was married and had my son, Max (age 2). Stephen was engaged. We all were very close and gravitated toward one another, especially since children were now in the picture. Mark, Stephen, and I all lived in Tribeca—walking distance to one another and to the World Trade Center. We often visited our parents, who lived in Battery Park City, and we all vacationed in our favorite beach town, which we considered a home away from home, Montauk, near the end of Long Island. My brothers and I were beginning our "grown-up" married lives. It was an exceptional time, very special and full of fond memories.

Jean and Max take their daily walk to the World
Financial Center, NYC, circa 1999.

CHAPTER 2

That Day: September 11th— A Morning of Confusion and Terror

My husband, son, and I lived on floor twenty-seven, a few blocks from the World Trade Center. We had incredible views; to the northwest was New Jersey, and to the east, Tribeca and downtown in all its glory. We also had a clear view of the Twin Towers. In fact I used to talk to Stephen, who worked on floor 104 of the North Tower, on the phone and tell him to wave to us; we could not actually see him, but we'd wave back. My son always got a kick out of that. It was a running joke between my brother and me.

That morning, we woke up at 7:30am, I decided to put Max in his stroller and take him out for some fresh air. The weather reports called for clear skies, and it was about sixty-eight degrees. Perfect weather!

The area we lived in was so beautiful, with only a few apartment buildings in what's known as North Battery Park, in the year 2001, and not overcrowded, especially at this hour. Max and I exited our newly built apartment building and made our way south along the Hudson River. The new esplanade was the smoothest and most direct footpath that led to the south tip of Manhattan. To the east of us were several other apartment buildings, a new baseball field, and a playground, while the amazing

9

Hudson, glistening, was to our west. Max, in his stroller, was taking in the sounds and the sights of the giant Colgate clock in Jersey City across the river, with joggers and Rollerbladers passing by. The sky was crystal clear, so blue. My husband and I had just returned from my best friend's wedding in California two days before, and I was in great spirits. It truly was a spectacular September day in the city.

It took only ten minutes for us to reach the World Financial Center, an impressive addition to downtown. The center was comprised of a large glass atrium with palm trees, a very pretty escape overlooking the Hudson among the hustle and bustle. The men dressed in suits and the women in heels were hurrying to work. I bought a cup of tea and sat beside a palm tree while Max and I watched the escalators bring all the employees up to their offices.

After a little while, we headed home to have a proper breakfast, but first we stopped for a few minutes at the playground for a quick swing. We had our morning fresh air, and now it was time to begin our normal routine. As it turned out, however, that day would be anything but normal.

Sesame Street was on TV, entertaining my curious two-year-old. He had just finished his Cheerios and oatmeal and was happy and full. He laughed and laughed as he tried to sing the words with the cute little red character we all know and love. As he was in his bouncy, I wiped down the kitchen table singing, "Lalalala...Elmo's world..." As I bent down to pick up the last Cheerio at 8:45 a.m., I heard an unimaginably loud crashing sound—a sound unlike anything I'd ever heard.

I ran to the east window, toward the direction of the sound, to see what had happened. I looked down to the streets; to my shock, people were flooding the sidewalks. *Where are they going?* I wondered. *Was there a car crash on the West Side Highway? Is there a fire in the deli? At Stuyvesant High School? In my building?*

I kept looking down, not even thinking to look up. Nothing made sense; everyone was running. What could have happened?

Then, right then, I looked up. I stopped breathing—there it was, a gaping hole in the North Tower of the World Trade Center. A dark cloud of smoke emerged from the hole, along with a tremendous amount of flames. Pointing a shaky finger, I quickly counted down from the top. The Windows on the World restaurant occupied the top floors, 106 and 107. I counted down from there: 105, 104...ninety-seven. That's where the top of the enormous hole was—ninety-seven, I think.

Even though I was shaking uncontrollably, I managed to pick up the phone and dial. My father answered to my screaming and crying.

"What is it? Jean, what is it? Did Max fall out the window?"

"Dad, an explosion!" I screamed. I couldn't catch my breath. "I think it's a plane...a plane hit the building!"

"Jean, calm down. Calm down," my father pleaded with me. "Which building?"

"A plane hit the boys' building!"

"Oh, my God. We're turning on the TV now."

I called my husband at work in Midtown. I was screaming and unable to calm down. When I finally did, I told him what I'd seen. A plane had flown into my brothers' building. He said he would head straight downtown.

As I hung up the phone, I thought, *I'm going to get them.*

I was barefoot and didn't even think to put on shoes or grab my keys or my cell phone. I just grabbed Max and hopped into the first elevator that arrived; I didn't even realize it was going up. An oblivious man was standing inside. With Max in my arms,

I looked up to see that the elevator was going up to the fortieth floor; I realized it would take forever to go up then down to the ground floor. I needed to get my brothers immediately. Clutching Max, I cried and crouched in the corner.

The man in my apartment elevator did not know what was happening and looked confused, scared even. I didn't even explain. With a desperate expression, I yelled, "I need to go down! I need to go down!" He hopped off the elevator on his floor and ran to his apartment, clearly afraid.

Finally down in the lobby, I could hardly breathe, but I was determined to save Mark and Stephen. Surely I would make it to them, meet them downstairs at the World Trade Center. *There must be a stairway for them*, I thought. *I'll take them back to my apartment; they'll be OK. After all, the plane didn't hit their floor. They're safe.*

Everything was happening in slow motion as I headed to the front door of the apartment building. Seeing that I was out of control, the doormen urged that I not go outside; it was "for my own good," he said. I told him that I had to get my brothers but my neighbors insisted that I stay put and not go to the Towers. People were coming down to the lobby from their apartments; everyone appeared scared and highly confused.

A woman ran out of my building screaming, "The tower was hit! The tower was hit!"

"Get out of downtown now!"

"Get out!"

I couldn't leave downtown; I needed to be close-by when my brothers came down from their building. I refused to leave the area. I knew the people who were coming down from their apartments; they were trying to comfort me. My son was completely quiet. He was witnessing the unraveling of his mother; he didn't know how to process it and was very still and quiet.

I'd never been in such a state of panic in my life. I frankly didn't know how to react, what to feel, or what to do. Breathing became difficult, unbearable. I held Max in my arms tightly the whole time. More residents were coming down from their apartments and gathering, trying to make any sense of what was happening.

And then it came at around 9am...*another* crashing sound— a loud, horrible noise.

We all covered our ears, the fear running deeper.

"The other tower was hit! Both towers are in flames!" yelled one of the doormen.

This sent everyone into total panic for the next half an hour; men and women were breaking down crying. People were running up and down the streets. Everyone was trying their phones; trying to reach out and call anyone who might have answers.

Then someone in the lobby yelled, "The Pentagon was hit."

It was official. "We're at war," people all around me proclaimed, and I realized I was in the middle of a war zone.

People were exiting the apartment building and running north. Workers from the World Financial Center were evacuating en masse up the West Side Highway. I was still in the lobby of my apartment building, frozen—frozen with fear for my brothers first then for Max and myself.

At approximately 10am we heard loud roaring noises again. *No, no,* I thought. All of us covered our ears in desperation. It was like hearing a mountain crumble.

"The tower is coming down!" someone yelled. "It's falling down!"

What did that mean? The tower had come down? Which tower? *Oh, God,* I thought. *I hope my brothers are OK.*

We now were instructed by the police to immediately evacuate— to run, to get out before the other tower collapsed. We had to run for our lives. They were attacking us; they were bombing America. Other planes flew over—fighter planes, I think; they were so loud. They were going to have a dogfight with our enemies right above us. I was petrified, trembling. I thought the bombs from these planes would explode all around us.

Who are our enemies? I wondered. *What's happening? Where am I?*

Still clutching Max, I rushed outside, going along with the tide of people. I exited my building, running amid the crowd, almost being trampled. Suddenly I caught the first glimpse of the smoke that eventually would overtake the otherwise blue sky. I was going to die; a building was going to fall on me. Unable to cope, I froze. I shut down; the movement was too much. I collapsed to my knees with Max in my arms.

Just then two women simultaneously appeared out of nowhere. One took Max from me, while the other helped me up and hurried me along.

"We have to get out of here. Come on."

"Come with us. We'll help you."

I listened. I stood and went along; we walked so fast that my bare feet were getting scraped up, but we had to keep going. We walked toward the highway then headed north up the West Side with all the other people. I turned back, only to see a gigantic cloud of dust among flames and smoke.

Smoke, black smoke—so much smoke. It covered the whole blue sky.

"My brothers are in there, my brothers," I continued to cry. "I can't leave them."

The two women told me not to look; in fact they physically turned me so that I faced north, to just keep me looking forward. Police cars, fire trucks, and ambulances were heading south down the highway toward the scene. Sirens were the only noise I could hear.

And there it was, at precisely 10:28am, the loudest noise, almost like a volcanic eruption, the crashing of the tower, my brothers' tower.

My brothers' building was coming down. Everyone—and I mean everyone—who was walking fast or running now stopped in his or her tracks. In one moment we collectively turned our bodies south toward the tower and watched it fall down. Slowly, slowly, it was crumbling. It came down almost in an organized fashion and in eerie slow motion. I watched as the tower—and my life as I knew it—came crumbling down. People gasped in horror.

Watching and knowing that Mark and Stephen and all their coworkers were in the tower was unbearable. I think my heart stopped beating; life stopped.

After watching the building come down in its entirety, the two women told me we needed to keep going, but no one knew where to go. All the streets were closed, and only rescue vehicles were allowed downtown.

CHAPTER 3

That Afternoon: The Towers Are Down; Where Do We Go Now?

We had to keep walking. My feet were on the verge of bleeding, but I knew we had to get somewhere safe. I didn't know what we could anticipate next.

We ended up on a side street, and I saw a Catholic church. Yes, I could go in and pray. I left Max with the two women, Wendy and Gloria, whom I'm convinced were sent directly from heaven. I trusted them with my life—and that of my son—and I hadn't even known them for an hour. I needed to pray, so I went in and knelt in one of the wooden pews.

"Please, please, Father. Make sure Mark and Stephen are safe. They have to be OK. Please, please, I know you're the Almighty. I know you won't let anything happen to them. And please take care of all of their friends. Please watch over them and keep them safe. Our Father, who art in heaven, hallowed be thy name…"

I finished praying and went outside, slightly replenished and able to move on. One of the women lived in the West Village, and we were able to get to her apartment. Once we entered, we collapsed on the couch and turned on the TV to see what was happening. It was at that moment, viewing the raw images on the screen, that I decided never to watch any footage of what happened on September 11th ever again, and I've stuck to that decision all these years.

Cell phones weren't working; no one could get a signal anywhere in the city. There was a landline at the apartment, so I called my parents, but they didn't answer. In fact no one I called in the city was answering. Where were my parents? Where was my husband? Where was my sister-in-law? Was everyone OK? Safe? Who could I call? I decided to try to call someone outside the city, someone on Long Island.

I called a friend, our family's real estate lawyer. He would know how to get in touch with everyone. Of course he had heard; everyone had heard the news. He was devastated knowing that my brothers hadn't been in touch with anyone. Jim promised to do his best to try to track down my parents and let them know Max and I were safe. Finally I got in touch with my husband. He was safe and told me what happened to him after I had called him with the news that morning.

He immediately had headed downtown to look for Max and me and intended to help my brothers when they emerged from the rubble. He was able to get close to the towers, but then the first one crashed down; he was in the cloud of dust, unable to breathe, and sprinted away from the building. Knowing my son and I must have evacuated the area, he went to my brother Mark's apartment south of Canal Street. They were ordered to evacuate, so he helped Mark's wife and my niece and nephew out of the area. They didn't know where to go; no one did. They called hotel after hotel looking for a room but were told no rooms were available. Even the hotels were shutting their doors amid the horror.

All the hotels they called said that if they hadn't stayed there in the past, they wouldn't accept them. June noted that she and Mark had stayed at the Pierre one night for their anniversary;

therefore, they would be in the system. She called there, and sure enough, she and her children were able to go Uptown and seek refuge.

My husband told me our friends would be able to take in Max and me at their place on Twenty-Third Street in Chelsea. I was to take my son and go to their apartment for the night. My husband would find a way to come down and meet us, which would be difficult since all the streets were closed.

After I got off the phone, I asked Wendy if I could borrow a pair of shoes. Unfortunately she had very small feet, and mine are very large. I didn't even fit into a flip-flop of hers. She gave me a pair of socks then walked Max and me twenty blocks north to Chelsea. On our way we passed St. Vincent's Hospital. I asked her if we could go in and inquire about Mark and Stephen; surely, if they were injured, they would be here, as it was the closest hospital to the World Trade Center. We walked into a relatively empty floor. I asked one of the nurses whether anyone had been brought in from the towers. To my surprise, she said with a heavy heart, "We keep expecting people, but they aren't coming." Then she looked down and apologized that my brothers had not been admitted.

When we left the hospital, among the crowd I saw a friar in his brown robe, adorned with a large cross. I went straight to him, and he opened his arms and hugged me. I was crying, and I asked him to pray for my brothers. He looked into my eyes and said he would. Then the woman and I, along with Max, kept walking north.

Eventually I arrived at my friends' apartment in Chelsea. They hugged me, and we were all crying at the shock and horror of the day. I was relieved to be at their apartment; they offered us food and drink, something I hadn't thought about all day.

I said good-bye to the wonderful woman who had helped me and thanked her profusely. I'll be forever grateful to Wendy and Gloria, the two women who saved Max and me. My brothers each had sent me an angel to look over us.

CHAPTER 4

That Evening: It Was an Act of Terrorism

My friends took very good care of Max and me. They fed us, gave us new clothing, and set up a room for us to sleep in. I was frantically trying to get in touch with my parents, my Uncle Jerry, anyone. At one point I looked out the window at the city; I could see the cityscape from the eastern windows. It looked so beautiful, all lit up with the clear, black, night-sky backdrop. After calling everyone on my contact list, I finally got through to my best friend's sister, whom I'd seen the previous weekend. She gave me the hope I'd been looking for; she told me one of the news stations had just interviewed a man who had come from as high as the ninetieth floor.

"A man climbed down ninety flights to safety," she told me, then assured me that my brothers must have made it down. I held on to that hope—a hope I would hold on to for days to come.

Eventually my husband arrived, and we all hugged and cried; we were alive and safe. Max was sound asleep. My sister-in-law, niece, and nephew were secure at the Pierre. Finally I got in touch with my parents. They had tried to drive into the city from Montauk as soon as they had learned what had happened. The bridges and tunnels were all closed, however, and they were diverted to Westchester, where my uncle lives. They were also safe and sound there.

Displaced and scared, my husband and I had no idea what was to ensue. Still we had each other, and we were grateful and thanked God. We were confused; what had happened? This could *not* have happened.

And where were Mark and Stephen? Why had they not been in touch with anyone? Surely they would be fine. They were with a bunch of amazing, strong young men who would know how to get out of that building; they would break the doors down if they had to. They must have escaped the burning building and be somewhere safe. At the very most, they would have been injured and taken to a nearby hospital. We tried to remain calm and make sense of this tragedy. That evening we had learned that President Bush declared that September 11th was an act of terrorism.

CHAPTER 5

The Next Morning: Our Temporary Residence

I woke up the next morning around six o'clock. It was a new day. For a second I didn't think of what had occurred the day before. Then I snapped back to reality—we were "at war," and I didn't know whether my brothers were alive or dead. Deep down, however, I knew they were alive. They were most likely in a hospital somewhere recovering, but we'd all be OK and together again.

My husband and I had breakfast and began another grueling, confusing day. Friends and family had tried to get in touch with us upon hearing the news. When they finally did, they gave us information they'd heard from the news reports. I couldn't watch TV since all the news programs were showing the Twin Towers coming down.

As I discovered, a terrorist group had planned the attacks on our country. This was the same group that had attacked the World Trade Center in 1993. These terrorists hijacked a plane from Boston and flew it into the North Tower. Around the same time, they hijacked other planes and crashed them into the South Tower as well as the Pentagon. I also heard another plane had gone down in Pennsylvania and supposedly had been heading for the White House.

New York City was on lockdown. It was extremely quiet since so many people had fled. But my husband and I had to stay; we had to find Stephen and Mark. So we thanked our friends and got in our car and headed Uptown. We had no extra clothes or possessions with us. On the way we stopped on the side of the road to meet my dear friend, Aine, on Manhattan's East Side. She was devastated, of course, but had managed to gather bags of clothes for us as well as others who needed them. We hugged and cried on the side of First Avenue as she passed my husband and me bags full of necessities.

We arrived at the Pierre and met up with June. My parents drove into town as soon as there was clearance and met us at the hotel. Everyone at the Pierre, especially the director of housekeeping, Ursula, was outstanding to my family and me. We started off with two small rooms. It was getting clear that more and more people were exiting the city, and eventually the hotel was able to provide suites to accommodate all of us. The manager made sure we had everything we needed. She was yet another angel.

CHAPTER 6

The Next Afternoon:
The Search Begins

While my family took refuge at the hotel, friends slowly started coming into town to help out. At this point the news of the event still was unfolding, and people were scared and confused. We still didn't know whether Stephen and Mark were alive. June's brother, Tommy, also worked at Cantor, and we had not heard from him either. That afternoon we all took separate stations in our suites to make phone calls. I was in the kitchen, my sister-in-law was at the desk, and others were in the bedrooms. We each had compiled lists of hospitals where Mark, Stephen, and Tommy might be. I called the New Jersey hospitals...nothing. Someone else called the downtown hospitals... nothing. The Midtown hospitals...nothing. The Uptown hospitals...nothing. Staten Island, Brooklyn, Connecticut...still nothing.

From their homes, friends were calling hospitals and clinics in Westchester and Long Island, but still there was no information. As far as we could tell, Mark, Stephen, and June's brother hadn't been admitted anywhere. How could that be? They had to be somewhere, mending; after all, although the city was in a state of confusion, people were attempting rescue efforts. We contacted the families of people who worked with Stephen and Mark. The conversations went like this:

"Did you hear anything from him?"

"No, we haven't heard a thing. We've called everyone we know. No word."

Or:

"He called from the tower. They were together, alive…but since it came down, we haven't gotten a call."

"OK. Thanks. We're at the Pierre. Please call us the minute they call."

That day, on the Internet, a list appeared that named people who had been admitted to area hospitals. The names were of individuals who supposedly had been brought in from the Twin Towers. Stephen was listed as "injured," and Mark was listed as being in "critical condition." With this news my sister-in-law and I hugged each other.

"They're alive!" we exclaimed. "Thank God."

My mother was very upset that Mark was listed as being critically injured, but we explained to her that all that mattered was that he was alive. "We'll deal with the injuries," I told her.

Around that moment, someone related to one of the missing persons went on national TV and reported that there were a number of Cantor Fitzgerald employees in the burn-victim unit in a hospital in New Jersey and said that two of the victims there were Mark and Stephen Colaio. The phones in our suites rang every minute; everyone we knew called us to tell us the miraculous news! We were certain they were alive now.

These reports, however, turned out to be false due to so much miscommunication and confusion. Our hopes ran high in one split moment then low when the hospitals maintained that no one had been admitted under the name of Colaio. We were on an emotional ride—up then down, then up, then down again.

CHAPTER 7

The Next Evening: The Gathering of DNA

Families were all instructed to gather any records for "the missing" as soon as possible. This included getting my brothers' dental records. It amazes me how people either help out in a time of collective tragedy (which I discovered most do) or cower and refuse to have anything to do with it. I called Stephen's dentist in the city and finally reached an answering service. When the dentist returned my call, I explained what had happened. I told him that Stephen was missing, that the authorities were trying to identify people, and that the only way to do that was by obtaining dental records. The dentist, who lived in Westchester, told me his records were in the city.

I said, "OK, is there any way someone can retrieve them so we can get a copy?"

"No, I'm not coming into the city," he told me, "and I don't expect to have any of my staff go in."

"This is of the utmost importance," I explained. "The city medical examiner is demanding the dental records of anyone who might have been lost in the towers."

To my shock, he was very abrupt. "*No*," he said then hung up. I couldn't believe it.

I then called our family dentist from our childhood years on Long Island. Without hesitation he had my brothers' records to me by the next afternoon. To this day it amazes me that the Manhattan dentist had no compunction to help, follow up, or offer any support in our time of need. But then again I have to remember people handled that day so differently; everyone was so scared.

Next was the DNA sample. It had to be taken from the nearest kin, a sibling, which was me. June's cousin Brian was tremendous in helping with this horrid task. He held up a cotton swab and told me to open my mouth. Then he took a sample of my saliva and placed the swab in a plastic bag. He included some strands of my hair in another plastic bag and marked it, "Jean Colaio, sister of Mark and Stephen Colaio, North Tower."

With my saliva, my hair sample, and my brothers' dental records, the coroner's office potentially would be able to identify my brothers' bodies if necessary. However, I knew this wouldn't be necessary, since they must have escaped, especially since they were so strong and smart. Or perhaps they skipped out and were down in the Caribbean, having the right idea to start life all over. That could be a possibility, no?

Our suite at the Pierre was news central. For those who could actually watch the television, they ended up being glued to it. These TV activists reported to the rest of us, who couldn't even look at a television let alone read a newspaper without hyperventilating. All I was interested in was locating my brothers.

During the evening there wasn't much to do but cry and pray. And we did a lot of that. We were all pacing, or lying in our beds fearing the worst, reliving the tragic moments, or praying to God. On this draining second day, we all managed to put the children to sleep, pray, then try to sleep ourselves, which was nearly impossible.

We tried to fall asleep, but it rarely happened in the days following, and doing so was still difficult over the next few months. Some people stayed up talking, yelling, even screaming with heartbreaking pain. My parents were in the adjoining room, and I'd go into their room and just lie with them. I stroked my mother's head; she stroked mine; and we tried to calm each other when needed. When she fell apart, I became strong, and when I lost it, she was there for me.

CHAPTER 8

Two Days After: Morning— The Most Supportive Friends Surround Us

On Thursday morning our hotel rooms were filled with chocolate-covered pretzels, bagels with salmon and lox, fruit, nuts, sandwiches, Pellegrino, soda—you name it, we received it from concerned friends. It was intended to "comfort" us. All very nice gestures, but none of us had an appetite. It turned out that our guests—our dear friends—ate the food, which was all right by us. We had morphed into an extended family of people helping one another take care of our children, our dogs, and ourselves. My best friends, Grace and Chris, cut their honeymoon from out west short to come help us. This extended family consoled my family, fed us, clothed us, and slept over if we needed them to. They were there for us 24/7, and for that I'm eternally grateful.

My former college roommates, Heidi, along with her husband Mark, Lisa and Matt, were stupendous, visiting us at the hotel every moment they could. They took the children to the Central Park Zoo across the street every day so we could attend the Cantor meetings to gather information and also so we could meet with others who visited us at the hotel. Along with our babysitter at the time, Dora—who was incredible as well—and my friends including Jill, Elissa and Ted, we'd figure out how to feed the children so we could determine what to do next.

Our city friends came over with huge shopping bags of toiletries and clothes as well as toys for the children. My husband was able to get downtown with the help of a friend who knew someone on the police force. They climbed up twenty-seven floors to our apartment on Chambers Street to retrieve some important papers, including our passports.

Marybeth, Kathy, Kerry, Michelle and Laura, June's friends and family, were there at every turn. Her siblings, Pam, Ray, and Anne who were experiencing their own grief over their missing brother, were extremely helpful as well. There was a tremendous support system within our two families. I truly don't think we would have survived without this special support. At this point I still had hope for all three of the boys.

CHAPTER 9

Two Days After: Afternoon—
The Cantor Relief Center

Toward the afternoon, after a night of no sleep, tensions began to rise. In the days following the attack, it wasn't all love and roses in the suites. More family members ended up staying at the hotel with us, and quarters were tight. We had cots brought in for those who ended up staying. People were snapping at one another, frustrated, with no answers coming from the outside. Hope began to wane every second we didn't hear from Mark or Stephen or my sister-in-law's brother.

Families who weren't used to one another's dynamics began to clash. We had to gather more DNA samples; the news was on constantly; and everyone grew more and more impatient, including me. We needed answers from someone, anyone. And all this was occurring during the bomb threats that were sweeping the city, the most frightening being the threat at Barneys department store, which was next to our hotel.

The greatest coincidence for us was that we heard Cantor Fitzgerald, the company where my brothers worked, was starting a crisis center right in the hotel where we were taking refuge. Surely this was a sign that everything would be rectified. We would soon all go home.

Not so.

I went down to find that the center had been set up in a huge hall. As family members arrived, they were doing something that seemed very peculiar to me. They were hanging up pictures of their loved ones with the word "Missing" on top. It was one wall, then two; then it felt like a hundred walls. I couldn't bear to look at all the pictures; deep down I thought all these people were safe and sound somewhere—they couldn't be thought of as missing. *Is everyone giving up already?* I wondered. On my way out that afternoon, as I was crying, a volunteer psychologist approached me.

"You look like you need to talk," he said. "I'm here to listen."

At that point I really didn't want to talk, but I started to relay my story anyway. Timidly I replied, "Where do I begin? My brothers were on the one-hundred-fourth floor in the North Tower when it was hit. We haven't heard from them, and we can't sleep or rest until we find out where they are. I was near the World Trade Center with my two-year-old son. I grabbed him and tried to go to my brothers to help them. But they…the buildings came down, and we had to evacuate."

The psychologist grabbed his collar; he started to sweat and appeared uneasy. Then he lowered his head and began to sob.

I was two minutes into my story when this trained, male psychologist broke down in tears. I stopped my story and consoled him and even hugged him. I recognized that he was only trying to help and hadn't expected to break down. At that moment I realized this was a tragedy beyond words. It was so fresh and raw that any New Yorker would have broken down and cried in an instant. At that moment I also knew I wouldn't be able to share my story with people for a long time, because it was so tragic that it felt surreal.

The director of Cantor Fitzgerald, Howard Lutnick, spoke to families of 'the missing' and gave out the latest information. I had met him and his family several times over the past couple of days. He had lost his brother Gary on that day as well, which put us in the same category of having lost a sibling. That was argument enough for me to listen to everything he had to say. I found his words to be extremely heartfelt, and he was a wonderful resource. He provided the most current news on the employees and the horrid situations. Even though he had the weight of the world on his shoulders, he came through with assistance and for all of the Cantor families of those affected. .

Different types of groups had started to form: the wives, the husbands, the siblings, the parents, the children, the grandparents, the fiancés, et cetera. People gravitated towards there respective groups who shared a disconsolate mutual suffering. People would retrieve information from the Cantor center and ask, "What group are you in?" I was a sibling.

CHAPTER 10

Three Days After: Horrible Discovery

The Sixty-Ninth Regiment Armory, downtown, had set up a place for family members to go with information about their loved ones. I didn't go myself, as I stayed at our temporary home, the hotel, to take care of the children, but I do remember that day very clearly. My parents went to the armory to find out whether there was any information about Mark and Stephen, or Cantor—anything. I was at the hotel with Max and all the others, still trying to call the hospitals in hopes that someone would be recognized or identified as Mark or Stephen or my sister-in-law's brother.

We were calling the hospitals when Jimmy, a dear friend of mine, phoned me.

"Did your parents leave for the armory yet?" he asked.

"Yes," I told him. "Why? Is everything OK?"

"No, Jean. I don't know how to tell you this. A friend of mine works at the medical examiner's office."

"Yes, and?"

"Stephen…Steve…has been identified. He's on the list of the first fifteen people who were identified as deceased."

I felt a punch to my gut. My legs went out from beneath me, and I collapsed to my knees with the phone still in my hand.

"That can't be true."

"He had his wallet on him," Jimmy explained. "He was identified from your DNA samples."

"That's not possible."

"It is. I'm so sorry. We have to get to your parents before they're in a gigantic room and find out with a ton of people there."

"I don't even know how to reach them. I'll have to call someone I think is there. What should I tell them?"

"Tell them to meet with my friend Sam and go into a private room. I'll have someone meet them from the medical examiner's office and tell them gently."

"Yes, OK." I was still, quiet even. I could hardly move let alone speak.

I went straight to the window of the hotel bedroom, which faced north, overlooking Manhattan. I placed my hand on the window, almost feeling Stephen's hand pressed against mine.

Later that day my parents returned to the hotel. They apparently had been brought into a private room for viewing the list of the confirmed dead. On that list approximately fifteen people were identified, one of them being Stephen Colaio. Their world came to a complete, horrible halt. They were distraught; this news single-handedly took the life out of them. They had no idea about my call with Jimmy. They exited the elevator at the hotel and went straight into the room.

My mother and father were devastated and told me to sit; they said they had found out some news. They told me Stephen was on the list and was dead. We were all hugging and crying, completely ripped apart. We were officially lost. Everyone in the room looked on with horror and were crushed. At this point there was no news of Mark and my sister-in-law's brother.

Any miniscule drop of hope that had been so needed had been wiped away.

Father Mark was our family's priest at St. Ignatius Loyola Roman Catholic Church on Park and Eighty-Fourth. The entire family had become close to him before my marriage in 1996. He had been a part of our family for a few years, performing or helping with all of our children's christenings at St. Ignatius Loyola. That was our church, where we felt most at home, where we prayed, where the most angelic choir sang, and where we performed our most treasured sacraments.

Father Mark came to the Pierre to help us through our shock and grief. Over the next few days, he occasionally performed Mass for us privately in one of the suites. On this night we prayed to God—about twenty-five of us, all holding hands—and asked for peace for my brothers, my sister-in-law's brother, and all our friends who had been lost that day. We all expressed our raw emotions and cried during our prayers. It was amazing that Father Mark could come and give us this gift of prayer. It was what we needed to get through those long, torturous days of the unknown.

He single-handedly helped my parents and me by talking to us and listening to us begin our journey of true grief. At one point I told Father Mark I had to keep praying for Stephen in heaven.

He corrected me by saying, "Oh, Jean, he is praying for you right now."

This stunned me. "For me?"

"Yes, he is at peace. He is looking over you and your family. He is the one praying for you and your parents to get through this," he explained.

I was in shock. I don't know what I was thinking, but his remarks were extremely pivotal in the beginning of my healing.

My faith teaches us to believe in everlasting life. My brother had led a good, decent life, so of course he was in heaven. My family and I were the ones left suffering in pain over his sudden death. We were crying for him, yet he was at rest. It was a miracle that Father Mark was able to be a part of our celebrations and now our tragedy. His effect on me remains profound to this day.

CHAPTER 11

Four Days After: Funeral Arrangements

It was official; we had to plan Stephen's funeral, a gut-wrenching task. My parents consulted with Father Mark and my Uncle Jerry about the Scriptures to be read and the music to be played for their youngest child. With pain and regret, they chose the most perfect passages and planned the Mass. Next would be the planning of the wake, which would take place at Frank E. Campbell Funeral Home. This was just the beginning of the hundreds of wakes and funerals for our friends and loved ones to come.

But what would we do for Mark? Would we wait for his body to be discovered? We knew they must have been together until the end; therefore, sadly, most of us had lost any hope for Mark. Although there were several different opinions in the room, my parents determined that we needed to wait to see whether we would hear anything about Mark. We would wait for days to implement the burial plans.

CHAPTER 12

Nine Days After: Final Good-byes

Even though there still was no official news about Mark, we knew we had to proceed with the proper burial of Stephen. The Colaios, with friends and loved ones, gathered at the funeral parlor and said their final prayers to both Stephen and Mark. This proved to be one of the most emotionally draining days of my life. Literally thousands of people showed up to pay their respects. Billy, Samantha, Aunt Antoinette, Aunt Eileen, cousins Tracey, Sean and Yvonne and more came from around the world, including Scotland, Ireland, England, Boston, and across the United States.

I was in shock by the number of people who came, but as I reflected later, this was everyone's September 11th. Of course they loved my brothers, but they, who also had borne witness to this tragic event, needed to come together and grieve. There were people from our childhood in Hicksville along with current friends and acquaintances. It was raining that evening, but that didn't stop the lines of people who waited for hours to come in and share their last prayers and wishes. Our dear friend Bob, who lost his own brother, Chris on that day, was tremendous. He knelt before my mother and grabbed her hand. A former marine, he shared how much he had loved my brothers and learned from them, and assured her they'd always be remembered and honored as great men.

The funeral took place the next day at St. Ignatius Loyola. The Mass is still blurry to me; I just remember that it was beautiful and emotional, and we were able to send my brothers off to a "better place." Again so many people who had an impact on our lives showed up. I saw many of them one by one when they went up to receive communion.

Our family left the church immediately to take the longest car ride I can remember. We split up into different cars and headed for Stephen's final resting place, a beautiful, serene piece of land that overlooked all of Montauk. We drove into Fort Hill Cemetery to find lines and lines of cars waiting for our arrival. Again I was amazed at the outpouring of love for my brothers. Our friends in Montauk helped with the planning and arranging of the burial.

In our religion the priest recites his prayers and dispenses holy water over the body-now-soul before the burial. The most perfectly magical setting surrounded us. Just as Father Peter (our Priest in Montauk) was about to sprinkle the holy water, a soft rain began to fall. At that exact moment, two Canada geese flew directly over us. Everyone turned around to look toward the ocean, and there it was: a rainbow. All at once there was a collective gasp. Father Peter said there was no need for his holy water as our Father had just blessed Stephen and Mark himself.

CHAPTER 13

Four Months Later: The Holidays

Thanksgiving weekend was excruciating. My family was still in shock and also confused as to how to handle the first of many holidays without my brothers. At this juncture, we still had not received word on Mark. News coverage regarding September 11th aired on a daily, hourly basis for months straight. We had remained in Montauk for the following months then moved into our new house on Long Island. I never returned to the apartment in Tribeca.

The manager of housekeeping from the Pierre, Ursula, invited our immediate family to come to the hotel and arranged for an intimate dinner in a room there. This was perfect, as we couldn't bring ourselves to cook or go out in public, since we were so heavyhearted. We all sat there, quiet, hardly speaking, fighting back the tears. When someone raised his glass to make a toast to the boys, we all started bawling. This would be the first of many sad holidays.

Shortly after Thanksgiving, I was invited to go to the site where the Twin Towers once stood. The city had created a viewing platform exclusively for family members of the victims. I went by myself and showed my identification to verify I was a relative. Everyone there was extremely respectful, and I was comforted by the fact that only family members of the victims were around me. I walked up the ramp to get a full view of what I describe as a burial site, also known as Ground Zero. The site and horrific stench were too much to bear; I cried and cried. A man came over and asked me whom I had lost. I explained, and through my tears, I asked him the same question.

"Heck, I didn't lose anyone," he said. "I just got myself on this family-viewing thing. It's much easier to see it all from here."

I was so angry! How dare he crash the family platform? There was a reason for this separation—we needed to feel the deep pain among those who understood best. Thinking back now, I can't believe I didn't say anything to him.

I was out to lunch when I got the call about Mark on a December Saturday in 2001. His body officially had been identified. We would have another proper funeral for him at St. Ignatius Loyola in January 2002. He was buried alongside Stephen in Fort Hill Cemetery, overlooking our favorite place on earth, Montauk. I had planned to spend some time at Ground Zero on Christmas Day to be with Mark but ended up not having to. Our family took comfort in this news and hoped others would be found as well.

CHAPTER 14

One Year Later: Anniversary Day

After much deliberation and questioning of everyone in charge, I decided to be a part of the memorial service of the one year anniversary of September 11th at the location now known as Ground Zero. The committee was looking for relatives of victims to help read the names of those who had perished. Until then I hadn't attended anything related to September 11th, except emotional support groups. I took the act of reading the names of those who perished very seriously. I purchased a red (patriotic) skirt suit and carefully placed my flag pin on the lapel. Then I put on my September 11th jewelry, which consisted of memory bands with my brothers' names on them, a rhinestone flag bracelet, a locket with my brothers' pictures, and a cross. I would wear this jewelry on a regular basis for several years after. I looked appropriately like a newscaster and planned to read the names with pride and dignity.

I walked into the tent where everyone who was reading names had a designated seat. Many people in attendance were related to those who had perished and others who were tied to September 11th. There were two moments of silence, one at 8:46 a.m. and the other at 9:03 a.m., in remembrance of the planes crashing into the North and South Towers respectively. Church bells then rang to mark the moments at 9:59 a.m. and 10:29 a.m. when the South and North Towers collapsed respectively.

I met many local political dignitaries, such as US Senator Hillary Rodham Clinton. When I introduced myself to her, she held out her hand and asked me whom I had lost. I told her, and with compassion she looked into my eyes and told me she was sincerely sorry. I was seated next to US Senator Jon Corzine of New Jersey, and we were all given a list of names to read. Then we all practiced the pronunciation of the names with one another. Everyone in that tent had a heavy heart but wanted to do a fine job honoring the lost by at least saying their names correctly.

Mayor Rudy Giuliani, appropriately, began the reading of the names. Then I went onstage and read my assigned names. It meant so much to the families to hear their loved ones' names— it was an acknowledgment that others were thinking of them; they hadn't been forgotten.

I proceeded to go Uptown to Central Park to meet my family for the Cantor Fitzgerald memorial, which was extraordinarily planned. It was a beautiful event. There were poignant speeches, live music, and a place where we could write a note to our loved ones. I felt that being surrounded by other Cantor families was especially comforting.

Cantor Fitzgerald First September 11th Memorial

That night at sunset, foreign dignitaries gathered in Battery Park for the lighting of the eternal flame at sunset. President George W. Bush addressed the nation from Ellis Island an hour and a half after the lighting of the eternal flame.

President George W. Bush's Remarks to the Nation; September 11, 2002; Ellis Island

Good evening. A long year has passed since enemies attacked our country. We've seen the images so many times, they are seared on our souls, and remembering the horror, reliving the anguish, reimagining the terror is hard—and painful. For those who lost loved ones, it's been a year of sorrow, of empty places, of newborn children who will never know their fathers here on earth. For members of our military, it's been a year of sacrifice and service far from home. For all Americans it has been a year of adjustment, of coming to terms with the difficult knowledge that our nation has determined enemies and that we are not invulnerable to their attacks.

Yet, in the events that have challenged us, we have also seen the character that will deliver us. We have seen the greatness of America in airline passengers who defied their hijackers and ran a plane into the ground to spare the lives of others. We've seen the greatness of America in rescuers who rushed up flights of stairs toward peril. And we continue to see the greatness of America in the care and compassion our citizens show to each other.

September 11, 2001 will always be a fixed point in the life of America. The loss of so many lives left us to examine our own. Each of us was reminded that we are here only for a time, and these counted days should be filled with things that last and matter: love for our families, love for our neighbors and for our country, gratitude for life and to the giver of life.

We resolved a year ago to honor every last person lost. We owe them remembrance, and we owe them more. We owe them—and their children and our own—the most enduring monument we can build: a world of liberty and security made possible by the way America leads and by the way Americans lead our lives.

The attack on our nation was also an attack on the ideals that make us a nation. Our deepest national conviction is that every life is precious, because every life is the gift of a creator who intended us to live in liberty and equality. More than anything else, this separates us from the enemy we fight. We value every life; our enemies value none—not even the innocent, not even their own. And we seek the freedom and opportunity that give meaning and value to life. There is a line in our time—and in every time—between those who believe all men are created equal and those who believe that some men and women and children are expendable in the pursuit of power. There is a line in our time—and in every time—between the defenders of human liberty and those who seek to master the minds and souls of others. Our generation has now heard history's call, and we will answer it.

America has entered a great struggle that tests our strength, and even more our resolve. Our nation is patient and steadfast. We continue to pursue the terrorists in cities and camps and caves across the earth. We are joined by a great coalition of nations to rid the world of terror. And we will not allow any terrorist or tyrant to threaten civilization with weapons of mass murder. Now and in the future, Americans will live as free people, not in fear, and never at the mercy of any foreign plot or power.

This nation has defeated tyrants and liberated death camps, raised this lamp of liberty to every captive land. We have no intention of ignoring or appeasing history's latest gang of fanatics trying to murder their way to power. They are discovering, as others before them, the resolve of a great country and a great democracy. In the ruins of two towers, *under a flag unfurled at the Pentagon, at the funerals of the lost, we have made a sacred promise to ourselves and to the world—we will not relent until justice is done and our nation is secure. What our enemies have begun, we will finish.*

I believe there is a reason that history has matched this nation with this time.

America strives to be tolerant and just. We respect the faith of Islam, even as we fight those whose actions defile that faith. We fight, not to impose our will but to defend ourselves and extend the blessings of freedom.

We cannot know all that lies ahead. Yet we do know that God has placed us together in this moment, to grieve together, to stand together, to serve each other and our country. And the duty we have been given— defending America and our freedom—is also a privilege we share.

We're prepared for this journey. And our prayer tonight is that God will see us through and keep us worthy.

Tomorrow is September the 12th. A milestone is passed, and a mission goes on. Be confident. Our country is strong. And our cause is even larger than our country. Ours is the cause of human dignity: freedom guided by conscience and guarded by peace. This ideal of America is the hope of all mankind. That hope drew millions to this harbor. That hope still lights our way. And the light shines in the darkness. And the darkness will not overcome it.

May God bless America.

By the end of that night, I was emotionally wiped out and rubbing my feet. I had just received word a few days before that I was pregnant. I was still experiencing grief, but now I had some hope and more to expect from life. The news of my pregnancy was extremely welcomed at this one-year anniversary point. I believed the news would help my parents heal as well.

On April 20, 2003, my twin girls, Catherine and Sophie were born. This was Easter, one of Catholicism's holiest days, one of resurrection. I had lost two amazing brothers, then after, God gave me two beautiful baby girls on Easter—a true miracle.

Mark and Stephen, circa early 1970s

Stephen, Jean, and Mark with their grandfather,
Ferdinand Colaio, former NYPD officer, circa 1971

Mary, Stephen, Victor, Jean, and Mark Colaio;
family portrait, circa 1972

Mark, Jean, and Stephen;
New York City; September 1998

Stephen and Mark at the Plaza; New York City; October 5, 1996

PART TWO

Reflections

Reflections

◆ There are good people in the world.

◆ There are evil people in the world.

◆ People grieve differently.

◆ Different groups form during grieving.

◆ Many people have been struck by tragedy in some way.

◆ Faith ultimately can get you through.

◆ Good can come from tragedy.

There Are Good People in the World

In the wake of this tragedy, I've witnessed the goodness in people. People offered their homes, clothing, food, time, donations, and hearts and souls to us. Support groups came together, and strong friendships were formed. I had believed people were generally good, and in this case, great benevolence came from many.

Two women, out of nowhere, rescued Max and me when they saw I was crippled with shock. They didn't even know each other, but simultaneously both saw we were in trouble. Wendy and Gloria didn't think twice about grabbing Max and helping me up.

Nurses showed compassion when they told me that no one from the World Trade Center had been admitted. A friar in the street embraced me when he saw I needed prayers. The Pierre took us in when no other hotel would. The hotel's employees couldn't have been kinder and made us feel as if we were a part of their family. My friends came to visit and provided emotional support. They stayed with us through the night when we asked them not to leave. They took the children to the zoo every day to give us time to make calls. They shopped for basic necessities and toys for the children, and gave us clothes when we had none.

When we were still evacuated and I was shopping for clothes for the first funeral, the manager at Saks Fifth Avenue heard about my circumstances and, on behalf of the store, credited me back every cent. From around the world, our family received letters, notes, prayers, quilts, and drawings—all labors of love—and support. We met countless volunteers from the Red Cross and others who were invaluable.

I appreciate the efforts of the first responders, fire fighters, police officers, and EMTs who went into the cloud that day. Their actions were heroic.

There Are Evil People in the World

Contrary to the good was, of course, the bad. I still cannot fully comprehend how the terrorist group planned to kill thousands of innocent people. They succeeded in killing, on our land, approximately three thousand people in a matter of an hour and were plotting to kill more. They murdered my brothers. My brothers did not "pass away"; they were killed. For both Stephen and Mark, we checked the "homicide" box on the death-certificate form as the cause of death. In the beginning I did not harbor anger, believe it or not. I was so distraught and heavyhearted that my anger had not yet emerged. I even told myself it was not the fault of the terrorists; they simply had been brainwashed as children and were raised to kill.

I waver back and forth with that notion. However, since that day, I've seen other acts of evil in the world. I heard some people were cheering in the streets when the planes hit. There's no rationalizing how a person becomes evil. It can happen on a global scale through terrorism or murder, as well as every day in one's own neighborhood. I'm now convinced evil is something within a person and very much exists.

People Grieve Differently

What do you do each year on September 11th? This can be answered a thousand different ways for the simple reason that everyone grieves in his or her own way. Family, friends, and relatives all have their own ideas regarding how to show emotions. And this can change drastically every year.

Some people became very judgmental: Why won't she attend the ceremony? Why doesn't he visit the grave? Why is she so private? Why are they so public?

Again everyone handles death differently, even within a family. I learned this the hard way, and to confess, I judged too. September 11th was such a public event that there are many choices regarding how, when, and where to grieve each year.

I always make the final call as to what I'll do, right up to the morning of the anniversary. The anticipation of the day is worse than the day itself. The weeks leading up to September 11th each year are filled with media reminders of the worst day of my life, which brings back the anxiety and feelings of fear. I, of course, turn off the television and turn my head when I see the newspapers at the supermarket. I gain solace by visiting my brothers' graves in Montauk a few times a year; I actually feel "pulled" to be there. I know the gravesite is just a physical symbol, and their souls are above, but Montauk gives me a place to express the sadness. I'll sometimes talk to them, and sometimes I'll just be with them and take a book and read in peace with them. I mostly pray. My choice to do that is a personal one.

Attending the Cantor Fitzgerald memorials on the anniversary of September 11th is a personal choice as well. I feel comfort being with others who are in the same situation; it's an unspoken understanding. We all suffered through the confusion, hope, and despair on that day and for years to follow. Every family has different dynamics, yet I believe there's a September 11th family. We have the opportunity to come together at these events; it's a bittersweet overture. Our brothers, sisters, mothers, fathers, and friends all worked together at Cantor and perished together. There's a comfort and a pull to the darkness all at once. Although I love seeing old friends at the event, it's heart wrenching when the names of those who are gone are announced one by one. Of course I focus on my brothers, but it hits me like a punch to the stomach that so many people we knew and loved were lost on that day.

Different Groups Form during Grieving

Many different survivor groups formed within this community: parents, widows, children, fiancés, domestic partners, and siblings. Among all the groups formed in the September 11th community, I obviously was officially in the sibling group. Many therapeutic groups formed in the areas surrounding New York City; there wasn't a specific group formed until later. I was a part of the Cantor Agency desk support group, which was mainly comprised of widows; there also were some parents and few siblings of those who perished. I'd known many of these people for years and felt a bond with several of the women. After a few sessions, however, I knew I didn't belong in this group; I had different issues as a sibling. In my eyes this is the worst kind of tragedy for parents. A parent losing a child doesn't follow the order of nature. I did listen to the widows and had compassion for their situations.

It wasn't until I attended a support group for siblings that I felt completely understood. I happened to meet a woman, Danielle, whom I immediately bonded with and with whom I know I'll have a relationship and understanding for the rest of my life. She had suffered the loss of her only brother, Doug, on September 11th. During the first meeting, we all introduced ourselves and told the group a little about the sibling we had lost. When it was my turn, through tears I said, "Hello. My name is Jean. I lost my two brothers…"

A gasp filled the room.

"Oh, my God, *two*?" people said in horror.

"Yes, both my brothers, Mark and Stephen. They worked at Cantor together."

"You have other brothers and sisters, right?" This inevitably would be asked.

"No."

Gasps again.

It was not until I received a phone call six months later from someone I did not know that I truly felt understood. The voice on the phone started, "You don't know me but…"

Kathy said she had lost her two brothers, Joe and Danny, who had worked at Cantor, and she was having a difficult time coping and wanted to reach out to someone who was in the same situation. This phone call was life changing for me. She came over within the next few days so we could meet.

It was the first time I was actually listening to everything I was thinking. When she told the story of how close she had been with her two brothers, it could have been me talking about Mark and Stephen. She too lived near her two brothers in her neighborhood. And she was saying the exact things I'd been thinking for months. It was such a relief and godsend that this woman and I developed a friendship in the face of tragedy—a friendship that's still very strong today. Danielle, Kathy and I were our own sibling group. There are other siblings of survivors with whom I have a connection. We have an unspoken understanding of the pain we, and our parents, felt and endured. We check in on occasion to make sure we're all OK.

Many People Have Been Struck by Tragedy in Some Way

When people know you've suffered a tragedy, they open up with their own stories. Many people have shared their stories with me. Some people I'd known for years opened up with their own stories. People can be quietly suffering all around us but unknown to us.

We don't know what people have gone through. The older I get, the more, of course, I experience—good and bad. We can't be too quick to judge; we have no idea what people may be going through. I have definitely learned to be compassionate before making any kind of judgment.

Faith Ultimately Can Get You Through

My faith allowed me to move from a very dark place to one of lightness. I understand that time heals, and there are the different natural stages of grief, but the combination of the two helped me with my grieving. I don't care which religion people follow—whether they're Jewish, Protestant, Episcopalian, Buddhist, et cetera. What's needed is some kind of faith that there is more than just us. Something more than us is out there guiding us, giving us belief in the ultimate peace, which helps with grieving.

Someone told me that when she attended my brother's funeral, she felt so comforted that the Scriptures read provided a belief in life after death. Her religion didn't teach that, but they explained that they preach the meaning of good and importance of support and traditions within their community.

At some point I went into a panic that there might not be a heaven. As a result I interviewed almost everyone I knew about his or her thoughts regarding heaven. I don't think I would have survived if I didn't keep believing that souls ascend into another realm. In general everyone I asked, from all different places on earth, believed in some form of life after death. Even just having the faith that friends and family will surround you during bad times is helpful.

In Roman Catholicism we believe there is everlasting life after death. According to the Gospel of John 11:25–26, Jesus said to the sisters of Lazarus, "I am the resurrection and the life. The one who believes in me will live, even though they die; and whoever lives by believing in me will never die."

We perform acts of good conscience on earth, and with the power of prayer, ultimately will bring us to a place of peace. Jesus rose from the dead on the day we celebrate as Easter. The fact that my twin girls were born at 12:15 a.m. on Easter Sunday, April 20, 2003, was a beautiful sign that my brothers were watching over my family and me. My two angels in heaven above sent two living angels to me.

Good Can Come from Tragedy

There were so many wonderful acts of kindness that day. The people in New York City were outstanding in how they rallied together and supported one another. If the September 11th families had an unspoken bond, the next level of unspoken bond was between New Yorkers. There's an unmatched strength to the people of this great city, and one needs this strength to get by here. On September 11th we were tested. Our city had been violated, in the worst ways, and New Yorkers weren't ones to sit down and take that quietly.

People with the Red Cross and other organizations came from across the nation to help the survivors. These volunteers had stopped what they were doing and come purely to aid those who had lost relatives and friends and those who had been displaced. I met a man from the Midwest who shared his devastating story of the loss of all his possessions during a flood. He came to New York to help others who felt lost and needed a kind hand. At first I thought, *He doesn't really understand what it's like to lose a loved one in this tragic way,* but then I realized there would be many who never would understand. They were innocent in not understanding, and I wouldn't wish someone to understand this kind of devastation.

Many charities formed after that day. In the year after the tragedy, my sister-in-law's family and friends began the Colaio-Pedicini Memorial Scholarship in honor of Mark, Stephen, and Tommy, who also was lost that day. This is a college-scholarship fund for students at Hicksville High School (the boys' alma mater) and a great way to honor my brothers and keep their memory alive. There are numerous scholarship and memorial funds for those who perished. Charities also were abundant for the families of victims. The Cantor Fitzgerald Relief Fund, headed by Edie Lutnick, is outstanding and still contributes to those affected by various tragedies.

One charity that stands out to me is Tuesday's Children, a wonderful nonprofit formed to help children who lost a parent on September 11th. Some of the programs they provided included a mentoring program for these young children, a take-your-child-to-work day, and career workshops for women or men who lost a spouse. Tuesday's Children also organized events for families to have a day of fun—for example Mets games for the children to attend. They continue to evolve and have reached out to the children of first responders and rescue workers.

Within Tuesday's Children, Project Common Bond is an amazing program that organizes children affected by terrorists from around the world to come together for a week in the summer to share their experiences with professionals and one another. Unfortunately terrorism affects the entire world. Now there's a place that provides understanding and compassion for others who have shared the same devastation.

My brothers wore "Life Is Good" T-shirts all the time. They shared these T-shirts with us, and when we were with them, they became our family's words to live by. Therefore, I believe right now, my brothers would tell us, "Life is still good."

Mark fishing in his "Life Is Good" T-shirt;
Montauk, New York; summer 2001

Stephen and Mark in Bruges, Belgium; 1996

Victor Colaio on Mark and Stephen's memorial bench
at Fort Hill Cemetery; Montauk, New York; 2013

PART THREE

Mark and Stephen Colaio Memorialized

Mark and Stephen were memorialized in many ways, both privately and publicly. New York City even has a street named after them, "Mark and Stephen Colaio Way," located in Tribeca, where they both resided. In Montauk, there are several benches in their names, at Fort Hill Cemetery, as well as at the Montauk Lighthouse, which my family and I have visited. There's a stained-glass window in their honor in the newly built Roman Catholic church of St. Therese de Lisieux in Montauk, and a plaque in their honor appears in the center of town by the gazebo. There also are public memorial sites where their names are displayed: the National September 11 Memorial & Museum at Ground Zero; the Town of Oyster Bay's memorial site at Tobay Beach (an area we frequented as children), and a memorial at Hicksville High School. There is a cross dedicated to Mark and Stephen in Westchester. There are scholarships in my brothers' names, including the Colaio-Pedicini Memorial Scholarship for students at Hicksville High School and past scholarships to the Boys' Club of New York. There's also a wrestling award at Lutheran High School in Brookville, NY in Mark's honor. My brothers have been written about in countless articles in *The New York Times, Long Island Newsday, New York Post, East Hampton Star,* and *The Hicksville Illustrated.* Their names, along with those of all who perished, are read aloud at Ground Zero every year on

September 11th. And there are a number of websites that allow people to express their love for those who perished.

It is with all these acknowledgments and tributes that my brothers' memories live on. Their spirit of good will not be forgotten. These places, articles, and honors for Stephen and Mark have helped my family in their healing process. My brothers grew up together as best friends, and they died together as best friends.

Of course, Mark and Stephen's true memory lives within me. Legacy.com, a website that allows people to let their loved ones know they miss and love them, was a site that I looked at during the dark moments to give me some comfort. This site gave me strength knowing that my brothers were missed and loved by many. It also gave me the ability to remember the good times and special moments shared by their friends and loved ones. Legacy.com helped in my healing of this horrible tragedy.

The following are some of my favorite letters written to my brothers on legacy.com.

Legacy.com Guest Book

Mark

March 12, 2013

To Mark's family: I know you can never hear too many compliments about Mark. I know it's always nice to hear from someone who was close to him. I had the privilege of being one of Mark's good friends in junior high and high school. And it really was a privilege and an honor for him to be one of my best friends. We played football from eighth grade until we were seniors. He always kept a positive attitude in any situation, and he really helped me out when my mother was sick with cancer. He's the type of guy that would put his arm over my shoulder and ask me how I was dealing with my mother being sick. He wouldn't take his hand away until I looked into his eyes and said that I was OK. He was always the life of the party and an advocate for bridging the gap between the athlete and smart student. He always lit up a room when he came in, because of his wonderful smile. Mark was one of a kind and deserved all the success he achieved. I wish I could share all the stories that we had together, but suffice it to say that Mark made my life better and gave me the strength to go on when my mother died. Mark, you may not be here in body, but I think about you almost every day and how wonderful your family must be. I hope one day I get to meet them.

—Basil

May 10, 2007
Dear Mark,

I just came across this guest book, and I was sure I had signed it last time. We were great friends back on the high school (LuHi) wrestling team....My brother Tom and I went to your memorial service here in the city. I still can't believe you're not here. Continue to watch over all of us from your perch in heaven. Much love to you and your family.

Your friend,
Pete

September 11, 2006
Hard to believe that five years have gone by, Buddy. You are sorely missed, as much as ever.
—Bo

January 16, 2002
Brother, life was good, and you did a damn good job of living it! I will never forget the day you took my five-dollar sunglasses, or your famous one-run Aspen ski days. Those were some of the best times of my life. I wish those times weren't gone. Mark, you are sorely missed. Every time the line blinks, every time eSpeed goes down, every time I miss a trade because I forget and pick up your line...Old habits die hard. You're gone, but in my heart, I'm still giving you grief every day. I am completely certain you'd want it that way.
anonymous

November 09, 2001
Mark: I consider myself very lucky to have been your cousin. I will forever remember you with a smile. I have beautiful memories—we all do. God bless. Rest in peace.
—Shannon

November 09, 2001

Mark: Your kind and generous nature and the pride in your family that shone in your face will always stay with me. Thank you. God bless you and keep you...till we meet again.

Love,
your cousin Erin

Stephen

September 12, 2011

Steve,

You always made everyone smile and always made them feel comfortable and that they fit in, regardless of who they were friends with. I remember your smile and your laugh and how you made all the years in Hicksville Junior High and High School a nicer place to be. I remember one time when I was in band, and the football team was giving us crap because we were practicing, and you didn't participate. You just started talking to me and made me smile. You were never like anyone else. I still have a pic of you from Annmarie's birthday party, and I remember that night fondly. Rest in peace, Steve. You truly will never be forgotten.

Hugs,
Tina

June 22, 2011

The nicest guy I never really knew. He piled me and two of my friends (and a quarter keg) into his Suzuki Samurai and brought us to a kegger on one of the beaches in Montauk. He didn't have to. He was older than us, but once he remembered me from Hicksville, it was game on. I think about you most times 9/11 is mentioned. I know you're up there with your brother, making people laugh.

—Michael

March 30, 2010

Happy birthday in heaven to one of my very first friends. It's still very hard to imagine this world without you, because you made the world such a fun and sunny place to be. You were a one-of-a-kind person, and there will never be another like you.

God, I wish you were still here!!!

I will miss you always!!!

—Sue

September 12, 2009

This is the day that always gets me. I am not sure why. I thought about you—and some others—all day today. It was a good day; the kids got extra attention, and things were more appreciated. It still hurts so bad, thinking I could do nothing when I was right there. My first step in the other direction will haunt me forever. I am so sorry. You are so missed.

Cheers, bud.

—Friend

September 11, 2003

Another year has gone by since you left this world, and somehow it seems as if it were yesterday. It was an honor to call you a friend since the fourth grade. My thoughts are with your family today. Godspeed, my friend.

—Desiree

November 30, 2001

Stephen: Although I only knew you for a brief time, you will never be forgotten. You shed such a bright light on people's lives, and your brilliant sense of humor could bring a smile to anyone's face.

There is a picture of you with Shannon and me at my wedding that we will forever cherish. You will be greatly missed. Until another day.
    —Scott
    p.s. I'll have a cigar for you

November 09, 2001
    Stephen: You will be missed more than words can express. I loved your smile; you were always so "full of piss and vinegar," as my dad, Uncle Joe, always said. I envision you now arm in arm with Mark, smoking cigars and playing cards with Uncle Joe. God bless you all. So long for now, handsome.
    Love,
    your cousin Shannon

December 3, 2001
    Although we didn't get to see Stephen, Mark, Jean, Auntie Chris, and Uncle Victor as much as we all would've liked because of our distance and busy lives, you are all such an important part of our life forever. Stephen, every time I would see you, I would be reminded of my dad. Whether it was your electrifying smile or your sense of humor that was so much like his, I always felt closer to him through you. He was so proud of you, Mark, and Jean, and though I was younger than you all, I learned so much about you through his stories and through his "infamous" videos (which we all seemed to dread!—but now will be forever thankful for and treasure). I miss you and love you. I think of you and Mark every time I hear the song "In the Arms of an Angel." It gives me comfort and hope, as I believe that you and Mark are in the arms of our forever angel, your Uncle Joe, my dad, and that he is in yours.
    Love, your cousin Bevin

Tribeca, New York City

Mary, Catherine, Uncle Jerry, Sophie, Victor, Jean, and Max;
Central Park, New York City; the tenth anniversary of
September 11, 2011

September 11th Memorial in New York City

September 11th Memorial in Hicksville, New York; 2013

Acknowledgments

Thank you to my parents, Victor and Mary Christina, the most honorable people I know; you've had to endure what no parents should. All my love to my children—Max, Catherine, and Sophie—who continue to inspire me and teach me about life every day; to my beautiful niece, Delaney and nephew, Joseph; and to my incredible Uncle Jerry and wonderful sister-in-law, June. Thank you to my college roommates, who remain steadfast; to my friends, old and new, who all have supported and inspired me at different points in my life. Thank you to the great team at CreateSpace for all your guidance. My prayers go to our armed forces, first responders and their families. Of course, my heartfelt condolences go out to all the siblings, families, and friends of those who were lost on that day.

Sunset in Montauk "The End", New York

Made in the USA
Charleston, SC
01 April 2015